LIFE'S LITTLE DESTRUCTION BOOK

A Parody

By Charles Sherwood Dane

A Stonesong Press Book
St. Martin's Press   New York

NOTE: If you purchased this book without a cover you should be aware that this book is stolen property. It was reported as 'unsold and destroyed' to the publisher, and neither the author nor the publisher has received any payment for this 'stripped book'.

LIFE'S LITTLE DESTRUCTION BOOK

Copyright © 1992 by The Stonesong Press, Inc.

All rights reserved. No part of this book may be used or reproduced in any manner whatsoever without written permission except in the case of brief quotations embodied in critical articles or reviews. For information, write to St. Martin's Press, 175 Fifth Avenue, New York, N.Y. 10010.

ISBN: 0-312-92927-7

Typeset by *RECAP:* Publications, Inc.

Printed in the United States of America

St. Martin's Paperbacks edition / April 1992

10 9 8 7 6 5 4 3 2 1

INTRODUCTION

Goody two-shoeism hangs like an angel's halo over the land, pressuring us to improve ourselves and constantly do the right thing. Recycling has us going around in circles. Sensitivity shades into silliness. One more rant about co-dependency and we will all go cuckoo. There are just too many good things to do.

Unchecked, the pursuit of perfection threatens to erase the little quirks and foibles and peculiarities that make us *us*. If we become any nicer, better behaved, more socially concerned, blissful — or repressed — we could end up a nation of ax murderers.

Enough already. The prescriptions and advice in these pages are meant as an antidote to niceness run rampant. The book points the way back toward sanity. Let each sentence be your clarion call. Think small and indulge yourself; vent your spleen lest it explode and splatter your neighbor. Go ahead and be a little obnoxious: make sucking noises; be pushy. Learn again to belittle, belabor and betray. Use more plastic, grind your teeth and experience again the exquisite satisfaction you once knew as a child when you peed in the pool. Our American way of life may depend on it.

Along with goodness, there is all too much gratitude in this society, but grudging thanks still must go to the following for their contributions: Victoria Gallucci, Lynne Ward, Gail Girardet, Gene Brown, Sheree Bykofsky, Paul and Chris Fargis, Dawn Sangrey, Bob Detmer and the one and only David Dinin.

1 ❖ Never tip more than a quarter.

2 ❖ Keep the chain letters going.

3 ❖ Post-date all your checks.

4 ❖ Hum along at the concert.

5 ❖ Take the hotel towel.

6 ❖ Signal left; turn right.

7 ❖ Help fools part with their money.

8 ❖ Don't keep secrets.

9 ❖ Pass the vicious rumors along.

10 ❖ Exaggerate on your resume.

11 ❖ Let everyone know how hard you work.

12 ❖ Practice the art of limp handshakes.

13 ❖ Hire a devious accountant; it's like giving yourself a raise.

14 ❖ Buy this book.

15 ❖ Read other people's mail.

16 ❖ Pay tolls with $50 bills.

17 ❖ If the mistake is in your favor, don't correct it.

18 ❖ Butter up the boss.

19 ❖ Talk with your hand over your mouth.

20 ❖ Misquote.

21 ❖ Tell the ending of movies.

22 ❖ Use sexist innuendos to get more attention.

23 ❖ Stand up your date.

24 ❖ Give little kids clothes for their birthdays.

25 ❖ Fire people by phone.

26 ❖ Sniffle a lot.

27 ❖ Never make your bed.

28 ❖ Cut people off in the middle of their sentences.

29 ❖ Slouch.

30 ❖ Wear jeans to weddings.

31 ❖ Leave the toilet seat up.

32 ❖ Add insult to injury.

33 ❖ Drive 50 mph in the passing lane.

34 ❖ Park in the handicapped space.

35 ❖ Take more than ten items to the express checkout line.

36 ❖ Fumble for change when boarding buses.

37 ❖ Borrow a book and dog-ear the pages.

38 ❖ Turn on your brights for oncoming traffic.

39 ❖ Finish other people's crossword puzzles.

40 ❖ Ask people what they paid for their clothes.

41 ❖ Rake the leaves into your neighbor's yard.

42 ❖ Pinch your spouse's love handles.

43 ❖ Don't sign your checks.

44 ❖ Mumble.

45 ❖ Develop a convenient memory.

46 ❖ Take personal calls during important meetings.

47 ❖ Take your boom box to the beach.

48 ❖ Remind people that their freckles could be cancerous.

49 ❖ Don't return phone calls.

50 ❖ Use the last square of toilet paper.

51 ❖ Ask people how much they make.

52 ❖ Don't flush.

53 ❖ Peel out. *Man!*

54 ❖ Leave a wet lollipop on the new sofa.

55 ❖ Tailgate the elderly.

56 ❖ Tell your kids to try even harder.

57 ❖ Tear articles from magazines in the doctor's waiting room.

58 ❖ Put sticky syrup cans back in the cupboard.

59 ❖ Let the phone keep on ringing.

60 ❖ Don't dot your i's or cross your t's.

61 ❖ Carve your name in picnic tables.

62 ❖ Leave your thumb prints on photographs.

63 ❖ Hold off paying the people who bill you without charging interest.

64 ❖ Send anonymous letters.

65 ❖ Drink from other people's glasses.

66 ❖ Develop a truly tasteless foul mouth.

67 ❖ Drum your fingers during other people's presentations.

68 ❖ Leave the concert during the solo or before the clapping starts.

69 ❖ Leave the price tags on presents.

70 ❖ Name drop.

71 ❖ Blow out other people's birthday candles.

72 ❖ Don't refill the ice cube tray.

73 ❖ Leave dairy products open in the refrigerator.

74 ❖ Don't leave a message at the beep.

75 ❖ Talk with your finger in people's faces.

76 ❖ Sleep until noon every day.

77 ❖ Smoke in bed.

78 ❖ Dress 15 years younger.

79 ❖ Forget to shower in the morning.

80 ❖ Be a day late for your anniversary.

81 ❖ Always be right.

82 ❖ Lean on the doorbell.

83 ❖ If there is going to be a fight, make sure you start it.

84 ❖ Don't take "no" for an answer.

85 ❖ Ignore "No Smoking" signs.

86 ❖ Bark orders.

87 ❖ Put coal in Christmas stockings.

88 ❖ Sneer at people who try hard.

89 ❖ Assume everybody agrees with you, but keep trying to convince them.

90 ❖ Brag a lot.

91 ❖ Leave your supermarket cart on the street or in the parking lot.

92 ❖ Pledge money that you won't be sending.

93 ❖ Leave bureau drawers and file cabinets open.

94 ❖ Don't vote.

95 ❖ Wash whites with darks.

96 ❖ Use gift wrapping paper a second time.

97 ❖ Crack your knuckles.

98 ❖ Follow the letter of the law, not the spirit.

99 ❖ Reserve compliments for people who can do you some good.

100 ❖ Treat underlings as such.

101 ❖ Argue with everybody.

102 ❖ Touch the paintings at the museum.

103 ❖ Get hysterical.

104 ❖ Block the entrances of elevators, buses and subways.

105 ❖ Insinuate, implicate and insist.

106 ❖ Threaten lawsuits.

107 ❖ Pass the buck.

108 ❖ Eat produce at the market; don't buy it.

109 ❖ Flaunt it.

110 ❖ Toss pants with tissues in the pockets into the washing machine.

111 ❖ Prevaricate, obfuscate and complicate.

112 ❖ Remember that your teenager is under 12 when buying tickets or paying fares.

113 ❖ Read *Winning through Intimidation* by Robert Ringer (Fawcett Books).

114 ❖ Gamble with the rent money.

115 ❖ Record over a borrowed VCR tape.

116 ❖ Tell people they are in your will even if they aren't.

117 ❖ Nurture conspiracy theories.

118 ❖ Don't get caught.

119 ❖ Ask for a rush job except when there is a charge.

120 ❖ Stay directly in front of or behind fire trucks and ambulances.

121 ❖ Cross at the red or the green or the yellow.

122 ❖ When giving directions, leave out a turn or two.

123 ❖ Dream up special requests for waiters and waitresses.

124 ❖ Every umbrella is yours.

125 ❖ Pry.

126 ❖ Don't make up your mind.

127 ❖ Practice passive aggression.

128 ❖ Toss things out the window: tissues, cigarettes, cellophane food wrappings and those sorts of little things.

129 ❖ Try whining.

130 ❖ Improve your posture by walking with your nose in the air.

131 ❖ Remind people who lose their job that they probably should have worked harder.

132 ❖ Accuse, confuse and refuse.

133 ❖ Prophesy woe, financial chaos and domination by Japan.

134 ❖ Leave the outdoor Christmas decorations up until March or April.

135 ❖ Talk with your mouth full.

136 ❖ Comment on weight gain in others.

137 ❖ Ask her if the diamond ring is real.

138 ❖ Keep a store of wisecracks for tense and serious occasions.

139 ❖ Pound the table.

140 ❖ Try the expert trail the day you first put on skis.

141 ❖ Scratch your pits whenever you want.

142 ❖ If it feels good, do it.

143 ❖ Answer a question with a question.

144 ❖ See what it takes to get the lifeguard to blow the whistle.

145 ❖ Serve corn on the cob to people with dentures.

146 ❖ Don't give to charities unless you get something back.

147 ❖ If you have to give blood, at least make a big show of it.

148 ❖ Have your secretary do all your personal shopping.

149 ❖ Ask the stewardess a question every five minutes or so.

150 ❖ Assume that your place is next to the hostess.

151 ❖ Add the straw that breaks the camel's back.

152 ❖ Clean your fingernails at the dinner table.

153 ❖ Take but don't give phone messages.

154 ❖ Stopping for red lights after midnight is a waste of precious time.

155 ❖ Tuck a twenty dollar bill or two in with your driver's license so the trooper will catch the hint.

156 ❖ Tell people what you think they want to hear.

157 ❖ Notice good ideas and pass them off as your own.

158 ❖ Smuggle a little.

159 ❖ Put the gals in the office in charge of the coffee.

160 ❖ Make jokes about terrorists at the boarding gate.

161 ❖ See if you can be the first one off the plane even if you are sitting by the window.

162 ❖ Put a title like Senator or Doctor before your name when making dinner and hotel reservations.

163 ❖ Balance the checkbook every six months or so.

164 ❖ Have an alias and the IDs to prove it.

165 ❖ Keep two sets of books.

166 ❖ Don't volunteer for the back seat and never take the middle one.

167 ❖ Skip town.

168 ❖ Leave the lights on.

169 ❖ Before exiting the elevator, push all the buttons.

170 ❖ Give unsolicited advice.

171 ❖ Don't do anything until you have been asked twice.

172 ❖ Put off until tomorrow whatever you can do the day after tomorrow.

173 ❖ Spot test "Wet Paint" signs.

174 ❖ Say "like" at the end of sentences, like.

175 ❖ Don't shower after working out.

176 ❖ Go up the down escalator.

177 ❖ Develop at least three strategies for cutting into the front of lines.

178 ❖ Change channels without asking.

179 ❖ Underline in other people's books.

180 ❖ Goose the bride and the groom.

181 ❖ Call the wife "the little woman."

182 ❖ Lie about your age.

183 ❖ Tell people what you expect them to give you for your birthday.

184 ❖ If you can't think of something nice, say something nasty.

185 ❖ Slurp your soup.

186 ❖ Be judgmental.

187 ❖ Snap your gum.

188 ❖ Focus on winning and to Hell with how you play the game.

189 ❖ Squeeze the toothpaste from the top and, while you're at it, leave the cap off.

190 ❖ Free cable TV is only a shady electrician away.

191 ❖ Send smutty birthday cards to your in-laws.

192 ❖ Open umbrellas in crowded hallways.

193 ❖ Announce when you're going to the bathroom.

194 ❖ Read over people's shoulders on the bus.

195 ❖ Hold out until the other guy gives in.

196 ❖ Ignore deadlines.

197 ❖ Revenge is sweet; get some.

198 ❖ Borrow money from your mother-in-law.

199 ❖ When it says, "Reserved Parking," that means you.

200 ❖ Pad your expense account.

201 ❖ Take the labels off unopened cans.

202 ❖ Adjust your underwear in public.

203 ❖ Cover up your mistakes and pass the blame.

204 ❖ Borrow handkerchiefs to blow your nose.

205 ❖ Pinch all the chocolate candies until you find the one you want.

206 ❖ Curse the umpire at a Little League game.

207 ❖ When you're done with your gum, stick it under the chair.

208 ❖ If you do something nice, make sure everyone knows about it.

209 ❖ Bribe kids; they are easy.

210 ❖ Needle, meddle, coddle, diddle, fiddle.

211 ❖ Crash private meetings with a big smile on your face.

212 ❖ Read the paper during family meals.

213 ❖ Be a perfectionist in absolutely everything.

214 ❖ Put a too cute message on your answering machine.

215 ❖ Be ambiguous; it lets you work both sides of the issue.

216 ❖ Measure people by the money they have and the clothes they wear.

217 ❖ Leave your pantyhose hanging in the shower.

218 ❖ Dish it out, but don't take it.

219 ❖ Chew other people's pencils.

220 ❖ Support the death penalty for parking violations.

221 ❖ Get a backseat driver's license.

222 ❖ Apologize a lot but don't change.

223 ❖ Change the rules to suit your needs.

224 ❖ Lie to your therapist and sit in her chair.

225 ❖ Put your cigarettes out in planters.

226 ❖ Make your kids stand at attention every morning.

227 ❖ Wear T shirts with gross messages.

228 ❖ Leave your shopping cart on line at the checkout — then go shopping.

229 ❖ Pull the covers over to your side.

230 ❖ Leave wet towels on the bedspread.

231 ❖ Let doors slam behind you — in people's faces.

232 ❖ Clip your nails in bed.

233 ❖ Repeat yourself.

234 ❖ Repeat yourself.

235 ❖ Quote Adolf Hitler.

236 ❖ Don't know when to stop.

237 ❖ Tell teenagers how things were in your day.

238 ❖ Play office politics.

239 ❖ Vividly describe a hysterectomy when the entrée arrives.

240 ❖ Put things back where they don't belong.

241 ❖ Use the whole can of starter fluid on the charcoal.

242 ❖ Hold the elevator until you have finished your conversation.

243 ❖ Scrawl your signature on important documents.

244 ❖ Take your colicky baby to the movies.

245 ❖ Hand out your business cards at funerals.

246 ❖ Have belching contests in restaurants.

247 ❖ Clean your ear with your pinky.

248 ❖ Let your blind date know she isn't up to what you were told.

249 ❖ Make the same mistake twice.

250 ❖ Pee in the swimming pool.

251 ❖ Ride on the shoulder until you pass all the jammed traffic; then cut in.

252 ❖ Master and practice your best wolf whistle.

253 ❖ Wear large hats during the movies.

254 ❖ Wear golf shoes on newly polished wooden floors.

255 ❖ Chew ice cubes.

256 ❖ Leave wire hangers on the closet floor.

257 ❖ Always have an ulterior motive.

258 ❖ Push the panic button every other day.

259 ❖ Take the biggest piece.

260 ❖ Expectorate on the sidewalk.

261 ❖ Walk your pit bull without the leash.

262 ❖ Forget the pooper scooper.

263 ❖ Get up on the wrong side of bed.

264 ❖ Forget the punch line, but don't let that stop you from telling jokes.

265 ❖ Kvetch.

266 ❖ Race the old woman for the last bus seat.

267 ❖ Take cheap shots.

268 ❖ Comb your hair in the kitchen.

269 ❖ Take forever to find your word in Scrabble®.

270 ❖ Cause gridlock.

271 ❖ Remember that everything was better years ago.

272 ❖ Bring 85 things to the dressing room.

273 ❖ Play handball against the greenhouse.

274 ❖ Change your mind.

275 ❖ Glue a chip to your shoulder.

276 ❖ Blame the victim.

277 ❖ Put salt in the sugar containers.

278 ❖ Greet each new day with a growl.

279 ❖ Put your initials in wet concrete.

280 ❖ Crack the spines of good books.

281 ❖ Draw mustaches on posters.

282 ❖ Don't rewind videocassettes before bringing them back.

283 ❖ Dangle participles.

284 ❖ Exercise chutzpah.

285 ❖ Whistle a happy tune — over and over.

286 ❖ Walk tall, carry a big stick, and use it.

287 ❖ Give out other people's unlisted phone numbers.

288 ❖ Take money from your kid's piggy bank.

289 ❖ Install a siren in your car.

290 ❖ Serve TV dinners, wine coolers and cherry Twinkies on Thanksgiving.

291 ❖ Do unto others as you would never have them do unto you.

292 ❖ Have a penny, take a penny.

293 ❖ Be vague.

294 ❖ Grab someone else's taxi.

295 ❖ Walk very slowly, and make sure nobody can get past you.

296 ❖ Assign names to your body parts, like "winkie."

297 ❖ Put advertisements under people's windshield wipers.

298 ❖ When others are in a hurry, take your time.

299 ❖ Don't shovel snow from your sidewalk.

300 ❖ Chase ambulances.

301 ❖ Overstay your welcome.

302 ❖ Hedge and waffle.

303 ❖ Kick sand at the beach.

304 ❖ Serve fish with the head still on.

305 ❖ Touch strangers.

306 ❖ Guilt trip.

307 ❖ Fog up the bathroom mirror.

308 ❖ Tell how awfully big your hemor-
rhoids are.

309 ❖ Tell little children the truth about Santa Claus.

310 ❖ Hit below the belt.

311 ❖ Bite your dentist's finger.

312 ❖ He who has the gold rules.

313 ❖ Remember the Sabbath and sleep late.

314 ❖ Worry your mother.

315 ❖ Pick your scabs.

316 ❖ Change horses in midstream.

317 ❖ Let the crumbs fall on the floor, and the chips where they may.

318 ❖ Get up early and take your neighbor's newspaper.

319 ❖ Drive like a cabby.

320 ❖ Point out mispronunciations.

321 ❖ Sneeze in a crowded elevator.

322 ❖ Get into a heated argument about the weather.

323 ❖ Please feed the animals, especially Crackerjacks.

324 ❖ Spring back; fall ahead.

325 ❖ Open the casket for one last look.

326 ❖ Leave the alarm on when he doesn't have to get up.

327 ❖ Shake up the club soda before opening it.

328 ❖ Make animal noises in libraries.

329 ❖ Fart in cramped public spaces.

330 ❖ Never forgive nor forget.

331 ❖ Don't tell the committee that you canceled the meeting.

332 ❖ Ask how people are, but don't wait for a response.

333 ❖ Stiff somebody today, but only if it's undeserved.

334 ❖ Hunt on posted property.

335 ❖ Leave lipstick prints on people's cheeks and foreheads.

336 ❖ Assume the authority but not the responsibility.

337 ❖ Get your back up.

338 ❖ Think nothing of it.

339 ❖ Appease belligerents.

340 ❖ Don't stand during hymns and anthems.

341 ❖ Be generous with backhanded compliments.

342 ❖ Try looking down your nose at newcomers.

343 ❖ Find good things to say about Richard Nixon.

344 ❖ Send mail "Postage Due."

345 ❖ Swear 'til you're blue in the face.

346 ❖ Wait five weeks to deposit checks.

347 ❖ Borrow your roommate's diaphragm.

348 ❖ Live in a glass house and throw stones.

349 ❖ Procrastinate and someone else will surely do it.

350 ❖ Eat like a horse and make a pig of yourself.

351 ❖ Drown your sorrows by bending the elbow.

352 ❖ If you can do the time, do the crime.

353 ❖ Believe that numbers and stars influence the way your life works.

354 ❖ Use more plastic.

355 ❖ Put all your eggs in one basket.

356 ❖ Play with fire.

357 ❖ Split hairs.

358 ❖ Let slip the dogs of war.

359 ❖ Cut corners.

360 ❖ Drown yourself in perfume.

361 ❖ Never eat crow, hats or humble pie.

362 ❖ Fish for compliments.

363 ❖ Crack the whip.

364 ❖ Have bones to pick.

365 ❖ Dance fast to slow music and vice versa.

366 ❖ Cook everything with chili peppers.

367 ❖ Drink orange juice right out of the carton.

368 ❖ Burn your bridges and candles at both ends.

369 ❖ Call your spouse by the name of an old flame.

370 ❖ Heads you win, tails you win.

371 ❖ Get light bulbs from the hall when you need them in the apartment.

372 ❖ Pass on the right in traffic.

373 ❖ Put pennies in the collection plate.

374 ❖ Lean way back in delicate old chairs.

375 ❖ Make fun of all accents.

376 ❖ Don't sign your greeting cards.

377 ❖ Leave papers in the copier.

378 ❖ Rubberneck.

379 ❖ Neck and pet in public places.

380 ❖ Ask your parents and grandparents how much they plan to leave you.

381 ❖ Brush the dandruff off other people's shoulders.

382 ❖ Lick the knife before putting it back in the strawberry jam.

383 ❖ Suspect a plot.

384 ❖ Tell long, boring stories.

385 ❖ Be "in conference" all the time.

386 ❖ Pinch kids' cheeks.

387 ❖ Bitch, bitch, bitch.

388 ❖ Get into every photograph you can.

389 ❖ Have a "Clergy on Call" sign made for your windshield.

390 ❖ Slap people on the back.

391 ❖ Swear this time you mean it — really.

392 ❖ Whisper behind their backs.

393 ❖ Misfile everything, especially contracts.

394 ❖ Remind friends of stupid things they did ten years ago.

395 ❖ Bum cigarettes.

396 ❖ Park in front of driveways and hydrants.

397 ❖ Don't tear the edges off computer paper.

398 ❖ Let your nose hair grow out.

399 ❖ Don't clean the dryer lint screen.

400 ❖ Shave every third or fourth day.

401 ❖ Eat crackers in bed, and then move to your side.

402 ❖ Cover your living room furniture in plastic.

403 ❖ Mix up books on library shelves.

404 ❖ Pass stopped school buses.

405 ❖ Flash your Rolex, even if it's phony.

406 ❖ Tape-record phone conversations and use them later for revenge.

407 ❖ Feed the dog under the table.

408 ❖ Refuse to use the coaster.

409 ❖ Don't mow the lawn more than once or twice a season.

410 ❖ Buy it, wear it, return it.

411 ❖ Be unprepared for public appear-ances.

412 ❖ Ask if a present is returnable.

413 ❖ Overconsume and buy on impulse.

414 ❖ Tell people they have bad breath.

415 ❖ Keep your car moving fast near the sidewalk puddles.

416 ❖ Call friends during the Super Bowl to talk out your problems.

417 ❖ Copy copyrighted software.

418 ❖ Drink hot coffee while driving.

419 ❖ Don't tell vegetarians about the meat in the casserole.

420 ❖ Occupy a café table for hours with one cup of coffee.

421 ❖ Smell smoke often and announce it.

422 ❖ Keep saying, "That's nice."

423 ❖ Wear sheep's clothing.

424 ❖ Open old wounds whenever possible.

425 ❖ Brag about your new fur in a pet store.

426 ❖ Tell jokes at funerals.

427 ❖ Throw a loud party in the middle of the week.

428 ❖ Convince other people to take risks you wouldn't touch.

429 ❖ Eat out with friends and "forget" your wallet.

430 ❖ Be nothing if not critical.

431 ❖ Practice pulling the wool over people's eyes.

432 ❖ Don't call to cancel reservations.

433 ❖ Sulk.

434 ❖ Be known for your sesquipedalianism.

435 ❖ Quote proverbs in Latin.

436 ❖ Go topless or all the way on public beaches.

437 ❖ Put everyone on the speaker phone.

438 ❖ Play with marked cards.

439 ❖ Develop the skill of cutting people down to size.

440 ❖ Refuse to have a nice day.

441 ❖ Say "uh" after every word.

442 ❖ Write Dear John letters.

443 ❖ Step on the back of the shoe of the person in front of you.

444 ❖ Deception is power.

445 ❖ Alternately raise and lower your voice to make people question their hearing.

446 ❖ Keep asking, "Are we there yet?"

447 ❖ Belittle, belabor and betray.

448 ❖ Rain on someone's parade.

449 ❖ Use up all the hot water.

450 ❖ Beg the questions.

451 ❖ Find the loopholes.

452 ❖ Covet thy neighbor or his wife.

453 ❖ Bet a beggar double or nothing.

454 ❖ Don't knock.

455 ❖ Refuse collect calls from your family.

456 ❖ If you don't get your way, take your ball and bat and go home.

457 ❖ Clean up your boss's desk.

458 ❖ Hog the dryer at the laundromat.

459 ❖ Eat off your date's plate.

460 ❖ Drink your roommate's last beer.

461 ❖ Shave your legs with your husband's razor.

462 ❖ Use bug spray in the car.

463 ❖ Bite off more than you can chew.

464 ❖ Eat garlic just before business meetings and intimate dinners.

465 ❖ Indulge in character assassination.

466 ❖ Jiggle your foot continuously during job interviews.

467 ❖ Wallow in self-pity.

468 ❖ Never dust.

469 ❖ Make scary faces at babies.

470 ❖ Run amok.

471 ❖ Look over the repairman's shoulder and kibbitz.

472 ❖ Put your feet on the table.

473 ❖ Play mind games.

474 ❖ Recommend untrustworthy auto mechanics.

475 ❖ Buy and read supermarket tabloids.

476 ❖ Bite the hand that feeds you.

477 ❖ Open gift checks at the wedding and announce the amount.

478 ❖ Tell everyone that they should be in therapy.

479 ❖ Flirt with a friend's spouse.

480 ❖ Lie with statistics.

481 ❖ Say the coffee is decaf when it isn't.

482 ❖ Serve wine in juice or shrimp cock-
tail glasses.

483 ❖ Give distances in kilometers.

484 ❖ Tell a friend who has had a disaster
to look on the bright side of it.

485 ❖ Make fun of men who cry.

486 ❖ Leave your fly open.

487 ❖ Throw out the baby with the bath water.

488 ❖ Borrow money from friends and then deny you did.

489 ❖ Wear taps on your shoes.

490 ❖ Leave used dental floss on the bathroom sink.

491 ❖ Learn to recognize greenhorns and sitting ducks.

492 ❖ Don't show up after you offer someone a lift.

493 ❖ Bring a bar of soap to the health club whirlpool.

494 ❖ Disturb the peace.

495 ❖ Sit in the home bleachers and cheer for the other team.

496 ❖ Pretend you're listening.

497 ❖ Step on your dance partner's foot.

498 ❖ Don't back up your computer data.

499 ❖ Cast the first stone.

500 ❖ Don't call your mother.

501 ❖ Go all out to win when you play games with kids.

502 ❖ Never acknowledge anyone else's contribution to anything.

503 ❖ Serve red wine with fish.

504 ❖ Don't date business letters.

505 ❖ Jump to conclusions.

506 ❖ Be a bad sport.

507 ❖ Shake with your left hand.

508 ❖ RSVP on the last possible day.

509 ❖ Answer the phone with, "What do you want?"

510 ❖ Put the fork on the right and the knife on the left.

511 ❖ Leave people in limbo with Call Waiting.

512 ❖ Have one for the road.